Library Technology REPORTS
Expert Guides to Library Systems and Services

Embedded Librarianship: Tools and Practices

Buffy J. Hamilton

ALA TechSource
alatechsource.org

American Library Association

Library Technology REPORTS

ALA TechSource purchases fund advocacy, awareness, and accreditation programs for library professionals worldwide.

Volume 48, Number 2
Embedded Librarianship: Tools and Practices
ISBNs: (print) 978-0-8389-5857-5; (PDF) 978-0-8389-9421-4; (ePub) 978-0-8389-9422-1; (Kindle) 978-0-8389-9424-5.

American Library Association
50 East Huron St.
Chicago, IL 60611-2795 USA
alatechsource.org
800-545-2433, ext. 4299
312-944-6780
312-280-5275 (fax)

Advertising Representative
Patrick Hogan
phogan@ala.org
312-280-3240

Editor
Dan Freeman
dfreeman@ala.org
312-280-5413

Copy Editor
Judith Lauber

Production and Design
Tim Clifford, Production Editor
Karen Sheets de Gracia, Manager of Design and Composition

Library Technology Reports (ISSN 0024-2586) is published eight times a year (January, March, April, June, July, September, October, and December) by American Library Association, 50 E. Huron St., Chicago, IL 60611. It is managed by ALA TechSource, a unit of the publishing department of ALA. Periodical postage paid at Chicago, Illinois, and at additional mailing offices. POSTMASTER: Send address changes to Library Technology Reports, 50 E. Huron St., Chicago, IL 60611.

Trademarked names appear in the text of this journal. Rather than identify or insert a trademark symbol at the appearance of each name, the authors and the American Library Association state that the names are used for editorial purposes exclusively, to the ultimate benefit of the owners of the trademarks. There is absolutely no intention of infringement on the rights of the trademark owners.

ALA TechSource
alatechsource.org

Copyright © 2012 American Library Association
All Rights Reserved.

About the Author

Buffy J. Hamilton is the founding librarian of "The Unquiet Library" at Creekview High School in Canton, Georgia. Hamilton. She earned her Ed.S. in Instructional Technology and School Library Media at the University of Georgia in 2005, taught high school English courses, and served as an educational technology specialist for the Cherokee County School District before deciding she wanted to be a librarian when she grew up. She collaborates extensively with the teachers and students in her school to create learning experiences to foster students' information fluency and digital citizenship. In addition, she works with students to help them create personal learning networks, engage in inquiry, to produce and share knowledge, and to harness the power of technology. She shares and teaches through her work as a speaker, conference presenter, workshop consultant, and adjunct trainer, and through social media in her personal learning network and on The Unquiet Librarian blog.

Abstract

As librarians look for ways to infuse information, digital, and new media literacies into authentic research tasks in the context of content area study and passion-based information-seeking needs, many librarians are turning to the model of embedded librarianship to establish and foster collaborative partnerships for learning. At the root of embedded librarianship is the establishment and growth of relationships that cultivate trust, enabling the librarian to become a true partner in teaching and learning.

This report explores how embedded librarians can use free and low-cost teaching technologies to support and enhance participatory learning experiences in school and academic libraries. Case studies explore ways partnerships for learning were forged and the impact of these collaborative relationships on the understandings and experiences of learners of all ages.

Subscriptions
alatechsource.org/subscribe

Contents

Chapter 1—Introduction — 5
- The Scope of This Report — 6
- Embedded Librarianship for Transformative and Situated Learning — 6
- Cultivating Affinity-Based Learning — 7
- Notes — 7

Chapter 2—Skype and the Embedded Librarian — 8
- Partnerships for Learning around the Globe — 8
- Reflections — 10
- Conclusions — 11

Chapter 3—Case Profile: Zoe Midler and Google Docs — 12
- Challenges and Opportunities — 12
- Contextual Relevance and Teacher Support — 13
- Who Says We Don't Need Badges? — 13
- Results and Assessment — 14
- Conclusions and Reflections — 14

Chapter 4—Case Profile: Ellen Hampton Filgo — 16
- Embedded Instruction and Help through Twitter — 16
- Blogs as a Medium for Help and Student Interaction — 18
- Reflections on Student Learning and Partnerships for Learning — 18
- Best Practices and Suggestions for Implementation — 19
- Conclusion — 20
- Notes — 20

Chapter 5—Embedded Librarianship in a High School Library — 21
- Introduction — 21
- Collaborative Seeds — 22
- Google Sites and Wordpress — 22
- Symbaloo — 23
- Wikis — 23
- Netvibes — 24
- NoodleBib — 25
- Scoop.it and Curation — 25
- Reflections and Conclusions — 26
- Notes — 26

Chapter 6—Conclusion — 27
- Embedded Librarianship for Creating Enchantment — 27
- Using Virtual Tools and Practices in Embedded Librarianship to Address Digital and Participation Divides — 27
- Resources for Learning about Teaching, Learning, and Technology — 28
- Notes — 29

Chapter 1

Introduction

Abstract

As more libraries focus on relationships and learning rather than being the warehouses of "things," librarians are exploring how they can more effectively offer instructional services to meet the needs of their learning communities.

As libraries shift their focus from being warehouses of books and materials to being places of learning and participatory sites of culture in their respective communities, librarians are reframing their roles to reflect these changes. As librarians seek to raise their profile as instructional partners and mentors for learning, many are revisiting the model of embedded librarianship, a model that "takes a librarian out of the context of the traditional library and places him or her in an 'on-site' setting or situation that enables close coordination and collaboration with researchers or teaching faculty."[1] When librarians are able to embed themselves in a learning community, they are able to "demonstrate their expertise as information specialists and to apply this expertise in ways that will have a direct and deep impact on the research, teaching, or other work being done. Through embedded librarianship, librarians move from a supporting role into partnerships with their clientele, enabling librarians to develop stronger connections and relationships with those they serve."[2]

I would argue that contemporary and emerging forms of embedded librarianship go beyond demonstrating librarians' expertise and instead seek to "distribute" the library by helping novice learners (students) build expertise and to position the learning community in which they are embedded as a participatory site of culture.[3] Additionally, embedded librarianship should do more than help convey information to students; it should help students master literacies, processes, and skills that are part of what Dr. James Gee calls **passionate affinity-based learning**. What does this kind of learning look like in a physical or virtual learning environment or some combination of the two? According to Gee, passionate affinity-based learning transpires when "people organize themselves in the real world and/or via the Internet (or a virtual world) to learn something connected to a shared endeavor, interest, or passion. The people have an affinity (attraction) to the shared endeavor, interest, or passion first and foremost and then to other people because of their shared affinity."[4] As we'll see in this report's case studies, embedded librarianship provides librarians with the opportunity to support and facilitate the qualities and conditions needed for an affinity group or space for learning:

- The group is formed around a "shared endeavor or interest."
- At least some of the people "must have a deep passion for the common endeavor," and the "passion may be reflected in different ways."
- The emphasis is on production of knowledge, not consumption; there are standards about what counts as "good" production.
- Leadership is flexible and shared, and mentoring is a hallmark.
- "Knowledge in the affinity space is 'distributed' in the sense that different people know different things and can share that knowledge when necessary." Everyone brings different degrees and types of expertise to the community.
- "There may be some requirements for entry," but "the affinity space is not closed" and is organic. Different learning paths are valued and encouraged.

- Lifelong learning is valued as novice and expert learners both strive to seek and produce new knowledge.[5]

As information literacy becomes an essential literacy and form of cultural capital in today's world, embedded librarianship offers exciting possibilities for teaching these processes and skills within content area study over an extended period of time. Virtual means of instruction can supplement, or in some cases replace, face-to-face interaction and instruction. As librarians also take on more ownership of teaching digital and new media literacies, they are experimenting with best practices and tools for harnessing the power of social media and cloud computing to connect, interact, and engage in conversations for learning with people while offering support from afar. Such support can also encourage people to utilize the services of the librarian in a face-to-face setting. In addition, librarians are reconceptualizing ways to use free and subscription-based virtual tools for learning as more libraries and learning communities offer distance learning options.

At the heart of successful partnerships for learning is gaining the confidence and faith of those with whom we collaborate. Building relationships and trust with both instructors and students is essential for the success and sustainability of the embedded librarian model in any setting. By integrating the librarian into projects that meet people at their points of need, librarians and those with whom librarians are collaborating cultivate a more authentic and meaningful relationship, as all stakeholders learn from the transactions occurring in the project, course, or unit of study.

The Scope of This Report

The history and case studies of embedded librarianship in academic and special libraries have been well-documented in journal articles and books in the last decade. Librarians are often formally embedded in clinical medical libraries, among professionals in a specific workplace, in an academic department, and, to varying degrees, in core academic courses in which they support content area standards as well as instructional literacy learning targets.[6] In these environments, the technology used to embed librarians has primarily been virtual reference and course management systems (CMS) like Blackboard and Moodle. In these virtual learning environments, the librarian primarily provides instructional resources; answers questions via chat, discussion boards, or e-mail; and offers links and information on library resources. In many cases, librarians also use social bookmarking to provide links and give citation assistance. More recently, embedded librarians are becoming essential members of research teams in academic institutions.[7]

This report focuses on ways librarians are utilizing free or low-cost social media and cloud computing applications to not only provide services and resources to patrons but to also cultivate learning experiences that spark and sustain conversations that will prove transformative for both the librarians and their learning partners. The technologies mentioned in this report are merely media for the core of embedded librarianship: transactional learning experiences in context and the librarian becoming an essential node[8] in the personal learning environments of nonlibrarians. The technologies used by librarians to embed themselves in a learning community are most effective when librarians can see how "*SICTs* (social, information, and communication technologies) . . . are effectively built on personal and experiential knowledge and best translated into thoughtful targets during instructional design. Understanding the competencies of your audience, the resources available in your environment, and your own comfort zones as an instructor allows you to more seamlessly integrate pedagogy and technology. Developing actionable knowledge of instructional affordances enables you to recognize the potential of a specific tool or approach to 'fit' a teaching moment."[9] In other words, pedagogy and learning targets drive the use and integration of technology to support those experiences.

Embedded Librarianship for Transformative and Situated Learning

In his blog post "Beyond Mindless Progressivism," Gee describes learning ecosystems that embody "post-progressive pedagogy" and a particular thread of this pedagogy he calls "situated learning." In the case studies in this report, readers will see glimpses of these particular characteristics of Gee's vision of situated learning:

1. Multiple routes to full and central participation for all members of a group . . . organized around an interest and a passion to which the interest might lead.
2. Multiple routes to everyone learning to produce the knowledge, dispositions, skills, and tools necessary to sustain, extend, and transform the interest and the passion.
3. Interest kindles motivation and the desire to explore. The interest must then be channeled into a passion so that learners persist towards mastery via a great many hours of practice. Otherwise learners need to find another interest that will lead to a passion. . . .
5. Feedback is copious. . . . [Plentiful data through multiple media] across time is collected and used to [empower] learners, assess their growth and

development over time, and assess, compare, and contrast (for both learners and stakeholders) different possible trajectories to mastery, including ones that lead to innovation and creativity. . . .

8. All learners must be able to pool their [area of expertise] with other people's different specialties and integrate their [expertise] with other people's specialties by seeing the "big picture" to solve problems that no one specialty can solve. [In other words, the crowdsourcing of knowledge and problem solving is vital.]
9. All learners are well mentored by "teachers" and peers at various levels, as well as by the presence of smart tools and well-designed problem solving environments (both real and virtual). All learners must learn to mentor.
10. "Teachers" are designers of learning environments that meet all the above conditions and they resource people's learning in an adaptive and [authentically] responsive way [in the context of real information-seeking needs].
11. Direct instruction and texts are offered "just in time" (when learners can put them to use and see what they really mean) or "on demand" (when learners feel a need for large amounts of instruction or text in their [journey] of problem solving). . . .
14. Learners . . . [utilize] the relationships and connections among different types of skills and knowledge . . . [through multiple resources (human and nonhuman) and develop a better and more nuanced understanding of] the larger social, environmental, and cultural implications of any proposed solution to a problem.[10]

The model of embedded librarianship is a timely and relevant vehicle for librarians to embody and foster this kind of learning environment through their partnerships with other stakeholders in their learning communities. Embedded librarians are uniquely positioned to emphasize people and learning as the essential core of libraries through their work as partners for learning and through positioning passion as the spark for conversations for learning and establishing new communities of learners.

Cultivating Affinity-Based Learning

Through this report's case studies, we'll explore how librarians are using resources—both human and nonhuman—in nontraditional ways and delve into strategies for scaling out traditional best practices through cloud computing and social media. The diversity of the four embedded librarians in this report—a retired school librarian, an elementary school librarian, an academic librarian, and a high school librarian—reflects how flexible and adaptable these teaching technologies are for any learning situation or need. These case studies also demonstrate how embedded librarians can use these teaching technologies to connect with learners of any age, whether young children, teens, young adults, or parents.

These case studies will exemplify unusual and easy-to-replicate methods for positioning the librarian as a linchpin in a variety of contexts. As librarians seek ways to elevate their relevance in their communities in economically challenged times, embedded librarianship is full of possibilities for sharing our skills and knowledge with others in ways that are scalable to any library environment. We hope that this report will energize and inspire your work as practitioner and inform your vision of the possibilities of how learning communities can constructively create the text and narrative known as "library."

Notes

1. Jack Carlson and Ruth Kneale, "Embedded Librarianship in the Research Context: Navigating New Waters," *College & Research Libraries News* 72, no. 3 (March 2011): 167, accessed Dec. 11, 2011, http://crln.acrl.org/content/72/3/167.full.
2. Ibid.
3. Henry Jenkins, *Confronting the Challenges of Participatory Culture: Media Education for the 21st Century* (Chicago: MacArthur Foundation, 2006), 7, accessed Oct. 14, 2010, http://digitallearning.macfound.org/atf/cf/%7B7E45C7E0-A3E0-4B89-AC9C-E807E1B0AE4E%7D/JENKINS_WHITE_PAPER.PDF.
4. James Paul Gee, "Society and Higher Education Part 5," *James Paul Gee* (blog), Feb. 12, 2011, accessed Dec. 12, 2011, www.jamespaulgee.com/node/50.
5. Ibid.
6. Matthew Brower, "A Recent History of Embedded Librarianship: Collaboration and Partnership Building with Academics in Learning and Research Environments," in *Embedded Librarians: Moving Beyond One-Shot Instruction,* edited by Cassandra Kvenild and Kaijsa Calkins, 5–12 (Chicago: Association of College and Research Libraries, 2011).
7. Carlson and Kneale, "Embedded Librarianship."
8. "Nodes are actors in networks . . . that provide information and advice that help people make decisions or cope with problems." "Lee Rainie: Why New Media Are Becoming Your New Neighborhood," Project Information Literacy *Smart Talks*, no. 7 (June 8, 2011), http://projectinfolit.org/st/rainie.asp. See also Michelle Boule's comments on this idea on the ALA TechSource blog, www.alatechsource.org/blog/2011/06/becoming-nodes-of-information.html."
9. Char Booth, *Reflective Teaching, Effective Learning: Instructional Literacy for Library Educators* (Chicago: American Library Association, 2011), 72.
10. James Paul Gee, "Beyond Mindless Progressivism," *James Paul Gee* (blog), March 9, 2011, accessed Dec. 12, 2011, www.jamespaulgee.com/node/51.

Chapter 2

Skype and the Embedded Librarian

Diane Cordell

Abstract

Retired school librarian Diane Cordell is cultivating a network of learning partnerships around the globe to teach students of all ages the art of photography and digital storytelling. Diane shares how she established these collaborative relationships with teachers and librarians and how her role as an embedded librarian has supported passion-based learning and created virtually connected communities of learners.

The embedded model of librarianship incorporates a number of elements, including teamwork, content knowledge, accessibility, adaptability, and responsiveness. In order to function effectively as an embedded librarian, it may be necessary to step outside of one's comfort zone and experiment a bit.

In my professional life, I've found that Skype, a free software application that allows users to make voice calls over the Internet, is a very effective means of connecting with other librarians, teachers, and students. Skype made its debut in 2002 and has attracted an increasing number of users. Its audio and video capabilities provide a simple yet engaging way for teacher-librarians to become partners in learning experiences anywhere in the world. Users may simply talk, add a video component, or share their screen with others. The chat option enables them to exchange links and other written information.

Some librarians use Skype as an alternative to the expense of sponsoring a school author visit. They access the Skype an Author Network, locate the name of a participating writer, and make arrangements for a free virtual visit. Others librarians help their students find experts who can add authenticity and real-world experience to research projects. The flexibility of Skype allows for a rich diversity of interaction: between teacher and librarian, librarian and librarian, librarian and student, expert and student, or student and student. It is the perfect vehicle for creating conversations for learning as an embedded librarian.

Skype an Author Network
http://skypeanauthor.wetpaint.com

Social networking is a powerful medium for connecting "untethered" embedded librarians like myself, who are semiretired and no longer working in a classroom setting yet who want to remain professionally involved, who strive for continued growth as librarians, and who are looking to connect with classroom teachers and support learning experiences for their students. Through my online networks like Twitter, I'm able to interact with other educators. Contacts made on Twitter, an increasingly mainstream microblogging platform, often lead to invitations to "visit" libraries and classrooms via Skype. Though Twitter messages are limited to 140 characters, this service offers an easy way to communicate, share resources, and locate content experts.

Partnerships for Learning around the Globe

International school teacher Clay Burell initiated my first embedded activity on Skype. His Korean students were starting passion-based projects on a wide range of topics. They needed subject area experts, so Clay turned to his online network and recruited volunteers via Twitter. The student who contacted me was interested in creating a plan for an American-themed restaurant. We Skyped for about twenty minutes as I answered her questions about typical US recipes, and we brainstormed menu ideas. By looking beyond his physical space and expanding his professional team, Clay was able to offer his class richer, more authentic learning opportunities.

My next embedded experience involved another online friend and colleague. Terry Shay, an adjunct instructor at the Upper Iowa University–Waterloo Center, asked me to speak with his adult students in an introduction to computers class. These preservice undergraduate students had questions about libraries, research, and collaboration, which I was happy to address. It was especially gratifying to share information with this demographic since it offered me the opportunity to foster a positive attitude towards librarians at the very start of some teaching careers.

Skype has allowed me to embed myself as a storyteller and instructor with elementary school teacher Amanda Marrinan's students. Amanda Marrinan, who teaches year 2 students in St. John Vianney's Primary School in Brisbane, Queensland, Australia, is a teacher I met through another social networking site, Plurk. My visit to her classroom (see figure 1) was an interesting cultural experience for me, and seeing all the students in their uniforms reminded me of my own parochial school background. Because of the time difference, I've Skyped with Amanda's class only one time, although future visits are a possibility. It's easy to forget that not all children's literature originates in the United States. Sharing favorite stories with students in another country is a broadening experience for all parties involved.

The most intensive embedded experiences I've had to date involve two fellow librarians, Shannon M. Miller and John Schumacher. The three of us met face-to-face for the first time at the *School Library Journal* Leadership Summit in 2010. Although Shannon is a K–12 librarian in Iowa and John is an elementary librarian in Illinois, they began a partnership that essentially involves embedding themselves in each other's library programs. They Skype as needed, weekly at a minimum, to coplan and then coteach lessons. A typical instructional unit might involve creating parallel projects, then connecting and sharing visually on Skype, as they did on September 15, 2011, for International Dot Day, a celebration of creativity inspired by Peter Reynolds's book *The Dot*. Shannon and John have a collaborative blog, *Two Libraries One Voice*, to archive the products of this partnership.

Figure 1
Club Click

At the same time that these two young librarians were becoming an instructional team, Shannon and I decided to start a photography club, which our founding group of students named Club Click. As with John, Shannon and I are separated geographically, split between Iowa and upstate New York, but Skype makes our collaboration viable. As the lead teacher, Shannon describes the desired activity, and we set up a time to connect (always keeping in mind those pesky time zone variations). For example, at the beginning of the school year, I might use Skype's screen-sharing option to present a slideshow containing basic tips on photography to new club members. If any students have further questions or need additional information, Shannon arranges to have them Skype again during a study hall or after school. We keep Club Click resources and student photography projects on a wiki, where Shannon and some of the other librarians who have joined us, or plan to in the near future (John in Illinois, Jennifer Malphy in Wisconsin, Kathy Schmidt in Georgia, and classroom teacher Stephen Gagnon in New Hampshire), have their own pages with editing rights. Our goal with Club Click is to introduce photography as a useful skill while hopefully inspiring in some students a lifelong passion for capturing digital images. In a delightful turnabout, one of our Club Click student members copresented at a conference with Shannon and Skyped me in to describe our club and how it worked.

Two Libraries One Voice
http://twolibrariesonevoice.blogspot.com

Club Click wiki
http://clubclick.wikispaces.com

One size, of course, never fits all, and policies vary with each school. In some districts, students old enough to have Google accounts (ages 13 and older) are allowed to post their photographs directly to Flickr (an online photo archiving site) accounts. Other administrations prefer that the librarian or teacher in charge of the local club handle that process. Similarly, one district may permit identifiable students' faces to appear in public venues, while others expressly forbid this practice. It's possible to work within the framework of such regulations. For example, if children are not allowed to publicly share photos of their friends for a project, they can focus on objects, pets, nature, and so on and still have a rewarding experience. Not every library owns sets of cameras, but sharing equipment for a group project is an easy fix. In addition, many students have their own devices, including smartphones with photography capabilities. Learning how to use this technology is another useful life skill.

These connections with Shannon led me, in due time, back to our mutual friend John Schumacher. I have Skyped with his classes numerous times, sometimes reading to them, as I did recently for Picture Book Month, sometimes providing an appreciative audience for their stories and artwork. On International Dot Day (see figure 2), children in John's classes proudly displayed the dot compositions they had created on their iPads. I, in turn, produced a short Animoto video clip for them, featuring photographs of "dots and spots" found in nature (on a ladybug, butterfly, jellyfish, flowers, etc., even including my polka-dotted pink rain boots, much to their delight). For Poem in Your Pocket Day, we all shared favorite poems, taking turns reading and reciting them to each other. During a spring celebration, I showed students a collection of historic Children's Book Week posters, and then they read Peter Brown's *Children Make Terrible Pets* to me.

Typically, John, Shannon, and whoever else is planning to be involved make initial contact on Twitter or Skype. The ideas for projects come from various sources: a school's curriculum, John's extensive knowledge of children's literature, Shannon's love of art and illustration, or websites like Anita Silvey's Children's Book-A-Day Almanac. Once an activity is decided upon, John starts a Google Docs document to coordinate dates and times for participating librarians and their classes, with appropriate conversions for the variety of geographic locations involved. After the schedule is set, each of us adds the activity to whatever type of calendar we use. On the day of the virtual visit, all parties check in via Skype chat before the interaction with students is due to begin to make sure there will be no problem connecting that day.

Anita Silvey's Children's Book-A-Day Almanac
http://childrensbookalmanac.com

Figure 2
Diane Cordell and John Schumacher (a.k.a. Mr. Schu) collaborating via Skype

It never hurts to have a backup plan. In my most recent virtual visit with one of John's younger classes, Skype's screen-sharing option wouldn't work. Fortunately, I had saved the slides I planned to use as a presentation in Google Docs, and once I provided the link, John was able to run the slideshow while I added voice commentary. Other options would be to upload presentations to SlideShare beforehand or plan alternative activities to accommodate either audiovisual or audio-only modes.

Reflections

The students with whom I've interacted have, without exception, been enthusiastic and appreciative. The younger ones enjoy having a visitor who is there just for fun: no grades, no consequences, just sharing a story or some photographs, almost like a grandparent. Older students appreciate the egalitarian nature of our time together. Members of Club Click are co-experts; sometimes I share tips with them, other times they share photos with me. All ages like the "cool" factor of connecting via Skype.

While these interactions are satisfying on a purely social level, I'd like to think that they have many layers of meaning. Since I'm no longer working in a school district, my contribution to the collaboration is different, but just as real: I help to bridge not only space, but time.

I can offer these young people a window on another world, primary source information about the America of the 1950s through the present. My perspective is necessarily shaped by my experiences, and I'm able to relate this different viewpoint via stories, conversations, and personal mementos. Educators love to toss around the term *lifelong learners*; I am able to model that for students, letting them see my excitement in exploring new ideas and acquiring new skills. Our nation is getting grayer, and tolerance is a two-way street. Mature adults need to value the young, and children and young adults should understand that growing older does not mean withdrawing from life and learning.

One of John Schumacher's elementary children asked him why I was Skyping with their class since I was retired. He explained that Mrs. Cordell was still interested in libraries and books and missed having her own students. Retirees are a great untapped resource for schools, a vast living database of information and expertise. Those of us who choose to remain active in our profession must vigorously seek out opportunities for involvement.

Conclusions

I'm not a "tools" person; I'm a learning person. However, when I discover a way to extend and enrich my professional life, I hop right on board. Skype enables me to explore many of the facets of embedded librarianship. I can use Skype to build meaningful relationships, provide support, share—and construct—content knowledge, and interact at time of need. The technical requirements are simple: a computer with Internet access and a built-in or external microphone and (optional) web camera. Skype is free to download for computer-to-computer calls; there are additional paid options for connecting from your computer to phones or mobile devices.

Being an embedded librarian means integrating yourself into a classroom and becoming an essential partner in instruction. Once, this would have been possible only if all participants shared the same location. Now, thanks to options like Skype, there are no such constraints.

The walls are down. All that's required is the desire to engage and a willingness to step outside of your comfort zone. None of us are experts on everything, but everyone is an expert on something. Use what you've learned, and learn more in the process. The profession of librarianship is evolving, and rather than fear the change, we should embrace it.

It's not difficult to make yourself "embeddable." It's possible, of course, to physically insert yourself into a classroom or library. You might post on local library listservs or contact regional directors to explore volunteer options. I would strongly urge you, however, to consider using tools like Skype to broaden your horizons. This would not only offer more opportunities to interact in meaningful ways, but also mitigate some of every district's facility security concerns.

Once you've downloaded Skype to your computer, a fairly simple process, make your availability known. On social networking sites, if you see educators mention a project that interests you, ask if they'd like you to join them. Attend a conference—most offer discounted retiree rates and it's a great chance to travel—and make new face-to-face connections. Hand out business cards and contact information, noting that you'd love to become a virtual mentor. Be available, be user-friendly, be flexible.

Embed yourself in a classroom, in *many* classrooms. Make the world your library and be a librarian to the world.

Chapter 3

Case Profile: Zoe Midler and Google Docs

Zoe Midler

Abstract

Google Apps for Education is not only helping elementary school librarian Zoe Midler connect with students and teachers to infuse information and research skills seamlessly into the curriculum but is also serving as her new medium for educating parents and including them as part of the larger library learning community. This chapter highlights Midler's experience in embedding herself in and outside of the fifth-grade classroom through Google Docs to build students' fluency in the use of research databases.

Collaboration doesn't look the same for all teachers.
—Rebecca (Becky) Reed, Principal, Warder Elementary, Jefferson County Schools, Colorado

I think about Becky's advice, quoted above, when considering my approach to teacher/librarian collaborations. This one piece of advice made me realize that as a twenty-first-century teacher-librarian, I can't just hope that contextually relevant opportunities will come along, that I will get a chance to share my research expertise and demonstrate how to use databases. I have to be proactive and find ways to inject and embed my expertise into the teachers' instructional routines in a way that both complements the teachers' learning objectives and also establishes my brand as information professional. Google Apps for Education has provided me with a medium to achieve this goal.

Challenges and Opportunities

My school, Flagstaff Academy, has been a Google Apps for Education school since 2009. Staff and students have integrated Google Docs into their workflow, and assignments are routinely distributed via Google Docs (as shared documents or templates); consequently, faculty and students are aware of the collaborative power of Google Docs. However, I realized just this semester (Fall 2011) that collaboration in Google Docs didn't necessarily need to be limited to cowriting, editing, and comments; I began to see possibilities for interacting with students through instructions, directions, tips, and hints at the students' point of need.

How would this work? I needed a collaborative partner to flesh out this vision. Our fifth-grade team requires students to conduct a weekly "A to Z" homework assignment. Every week students answer a specific set of questions that include a topic that begins with a specific letter of the alphabet.

Many of the parent volunteers in the Library Media Center (LMC) are also mothers of fifth-grade students. I heard firsthand about their frustration helping their students conduct their A to Z research: their children didn't know where to go to find facts, and they didn't know if what they found was credible. I noticed that the students would type entire questions into Google and just use whatever sources came up in the first three results. Additionally, the students seemed unaware of Creative Commons (CC)–licensed multimedia or concepts related to copyright and intellectual property.

When I showed them our Safe Searching Resources (Facts on File, CultureGrams, e-books, *Grzimek's,* research guides [also known as research pathfinders]) and how easy it is to locate targeted facts using these tools, students were initially surprised to learn these resources existed and were available to them; they also liked the fact that source citations were included in these resources. Additionally, students enjoyed discovering how to find copyright-friendly multimedia by using the CC Image Searching page on the LMCWiki.

LMCWiki
http://flagstaffacademylmc.wikispaces.com

Parents and students who came into the LMC to work on A to Z would benefit from my guidance and suggestions. However, this method was hit-or-miss at best. I had to think of a way to reach everyone, parents and students, at the point of need. That's when I decided to create LMCTips and hints and embed them directly in the A to Z assignment.

I asked the fifth-grade lead teacher, Kelly Burnett, to share the A to Z weekly assignments with me. The assignment was a Google Docs document that each fifth-grade teacher publishes as a webpage to her website. Burnett gave me edit rights to the Google document so whatever I added would automatically update to the webpage and assignment. I completely rebranded the A to Z assignment, adding a logo to the assignment page and specific directions on how students could use Safe Searching Resources to locate data and information that would help them find facts and formulate answers for that week's letter.

Kelly Burnett's A to Z Weekly Letter
https://sites.google.com/a/flagstaffacademy.org/mrs-burnett-s-5th-grade/assignments/a---z-weekly-letter

Contextual Relevance and Teacher Support

In addition to adding LMCTips and hints, the fifth-grade team also scheduled class visits in the LMC for letters B–D so I could introduce how LMCTips worked within the document and model Safe Searching resource features and benefits. These benefits included

- accessing the LMCWiki (Safe Searching portal—one-stop-shopping)
- reviewing passwords for databases
- modeling the difference between searching on Google and searching for information in a database
- recognizing and developing keywords as part of search literacy
- discussing MLA7 citation format and the importance of citing sources
- demonstrating how Google finds results (ranking versus filtering)
- locating citations in databases and demonstrating citation builders

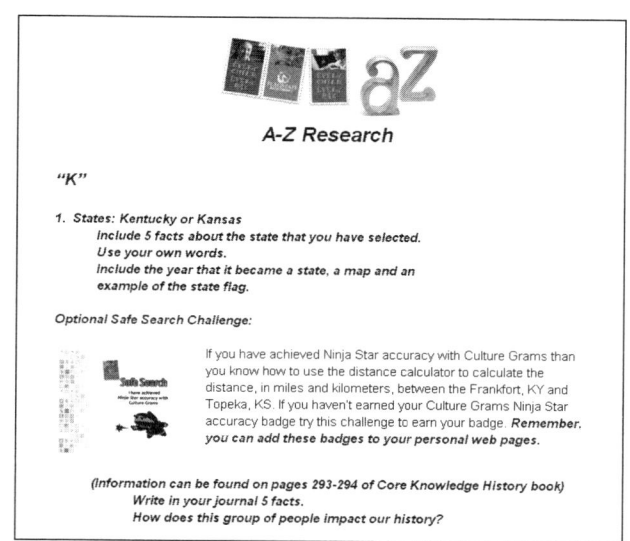

Figure 3
Sample LMCTip A to Z graphic

The teachers were present for every session and were adamant that students use the LMCTips, hints, and Safe Searching Resources for A to Z (see figure 3). Because teachers wanted to immerse their students in the database resources, students were not allowed to use sources through Google Search. Burnett created an A to Z citation log in which students are required to cite all sources they used for that week's letter. I embedded sample citations, a link to the EasyBib MLA7 citation guide, and links to popular citation builders into the citation log. All citations must adhere to MLA7 format, and if a student uses an open Web source from the research pathfinder, he or she must build a citation or use a citation builder to create an accurate MLA7 citation.

The other benefit of the LMCTips has been the opportunity to model searching virtually for students. If they repeat the steps outlined in the LMCTips, it's as if I am sitting next to them showing them how to search more efficiently.

Who Says We Don't Need Badges?

To further motivate students to follow the LMCTips, I created a series of virtual badges that students can earn to demonstrate their Safe Searching (database) proficiency. I embed an image of the badge into the A to Z assignment page. These badges really got the students' attention! To earn a badge, students share their citation logs with the teacher, and it is up to the teacher whether or not a student has followed the LMCTips and earned the badge. Once a student or class earns a badge, the teacher posts the badge to her website, and students can also post it to their personal websites.

Results and Assessment

Initially, a few students would come to the library and say that they were using the tips and finding helpful, meaningful information. I would ask then to show me what they did and ask questions like these:

- Did you follow the tip directions?
- Did you read the result snippets?
- Did you click on the right result?

In each case, I discovered the student didn't quite follow the directions and had fallen into the old habit of searching for information with Google instead of rereading the directions and steps for the search exercise.

Working with the fifth-grade team, we took a routine weekly fact-finding assignment and cranked it up a notch by adding specific search skill tips and providing virtual badges as an incentive. According to Burnett, "The fifth grade team has greatly appreciated Zoe's work on improving the quality of research for our A to Z project. She provides the students with resources that help them learn in a fun and engaging manner." Another fifth-grade teacher added, "The students have LOVED the resources that are added to the A-Z assignments. They are able to find more meaningful and useful information by using these credible sites."

Parents have communicated to teachers that they are using LMCTips to help direct their students. In the process, parents are learning the value of our Safe Searching resources and encouraging their students to use those resources first before heading to Google. One parent told me, " I get it, you don't want us to start with Google." Another parent, who learned how to use the databases side-by-side with her child, commented, "What fantastic information. I never realized we had access to such a vast spectrum of resources!" Because this initial effort has been so successful, Burnett and I are already planning on conducting A to Z Safe Searching workshops for parents at the beginning of next year so we can introduce parents to our collection of databases and e-books before students begin their research efforts.

Here are some reflections about LMCTips from fifth graders:

- "I love LMCTips because instead of being worried out of my head trying to figure to find info the LMCTips keep me cool & right on track!!" —Laura
- "They [LMCTips] help you get your A–Z done quick & easy. They make sure you not Google things too much." —Alak
- "I like the LMCTips because instead of looking everywhere I can just go straight to the perfect spot." —Brinley
- "The LMCTips help a lot by telling you some keywords and hints." —Andrew

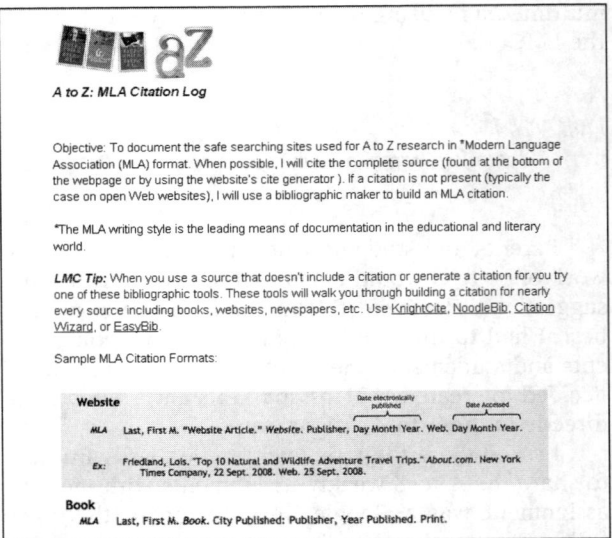

Figure 4
MLA citation log

Teachers and I are watching the citation logs (see figure 4) to see if students are correctly citing sources and whether the sources are database sources or librarian-vetted pathfinder sources. Teachers are also observing where students go to find information for other research efforts, for example, animal classification, explorers, and so on. Teachers and parents are saying that students are making the LMCWiki databases and pathfinders their first stop.

We are also watching our database usage logs and can see a direct correlation between database activity spikes and units of study that lend themselves to these sources. In the past, students researching states never visited CultureGrams, but now we can see a huge increase in visits and retrievals during this unit of study. The same is true for *Grzimek's* during the Animal Classification unit of study and for the Westward Expansion e-book reference collection during the Civil War and Westward Expansion unit of study. A to Z to was first and foremost about creating awareness of these resources and teaching students that there are alternatives to Google. We have achieved this goal.

Conclusions and Reflections

I am embedding tips directly into assignments and rubrics created in Google Docs (documents, spreadsheets, and presentations) that are shared with students or published as webpages on teachers' websites. I have also developed a suite of Google Docs templates for middle school students to use for their STEM Fair research process that include embedded instructions on how to create publication-quality formatted

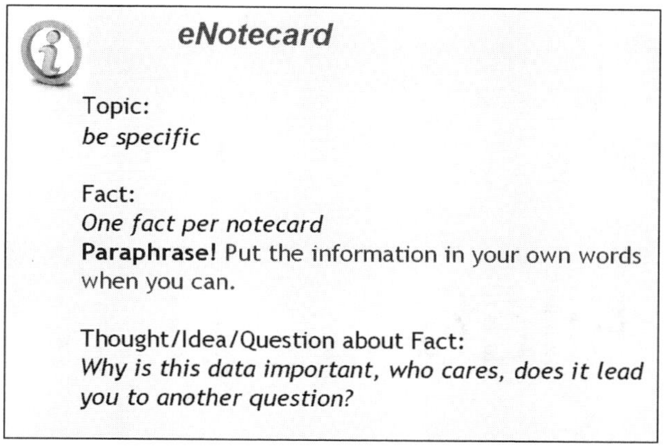

eNotecard

Topic:
be specific

Fact:
One fact per notecard
Paraphrase! Put the information in your own words when you can.

Thought/Idea/Question about Fact:
Why is this data important, who cares, does it lead you to another question?

Figure 5
eNotecard template

documents and how to avoid cut-and-paste plagiarism. Students in grades five through eight are using an eNotecard template (see figure 5) I created as a Google Docs presentation that includes sample notecards that students can duplicate and a keyword searching slide where students can list keywords and concepts as they research. Students share their eNotecards with me, and I comment or offer tips on their notes, provide more keywords, and send them direct links to database articles and additional resources.

I am not waiting for teachers to schedule flex time to collaborate, but instead I am actively seeking out ways to embed my expertise and our collection of virtual resources into the fabric of an assignment or unit of study. Google Apps allows teacher-librarians to reach out to teachers, students, and parents and provide instruction and help in a relevant and timely way.

Samples of A to Z LMCTips, Safe Searching Badges, and eNotecards

Letter D
https://docs.google.com/document/d/1IJhWpLFEmaZTNbkeK5NbONsQCayN2wXBXDdzpJOfCdc/edit

Letter E
https://docs.google.com/document/d/1ARwAMnaPZe67x6hpNL2VDZ_FxBBYZzAfHBWEXh5YAtw/edit

Letter F
https://docs.google.com/document/d/1PzSXjA0S5dJvA9BHPSQScIkb_uyFOlJ7EWnYFBvMTMo/edit

Letter I
https://docs.google.com/document/d/16f0RDSStoDfYAXvt8SFlpH4_egmjZzD49_DiwZSWmqA/edit

MLA Citation Log
https://docs.google.com/document/d/1OdqFYxEN4zhMAHJGunLXKemHF5F35B87AsUZaA04JDc/edit

eNotecard
https://docs.google.com/present/edit?id=0AXTMxa8a1N03ZHI2azV4aF82OTZjNDJrZzhmNw

Chapter 4

Case Profile: Ellen Hampton Filgo

Buffy J. Hamilton

Abstract

Ellen Hampton Filgo, an academic librarian at Baylor University, conceptualizes her work as an embedded librarian as improvisational, like jazz, as her instructional help and interaction with students plays off the class discussion in which she participates through Twitter and blogs. This case study outlines how Filgo became a vital resource for class discussions and research on a weekly basis in a first-year university honors course exploring new media studies.

Ellen Hampton Filgo is the e-learning librarian in the reference and instruction department of Baylor University Libraries. Her work as an embedded librarian at Baylor reflects her interests in the instructional uses of social networking media and ways libraries can use and adapt Web 2.0 tools to improve access to online resources.

Filgo's work as an embedded librarian began in Dr. Gardner Campbell's first-year honors seminar, "From Memex to YouTube: Introduction to New Media Studies," a class designed to explore a diverse range of digital media through many different contextual lenses. Filgo and Campbell's collaborative partnership was initially inspired by Filgo's viewing of Dr. Monica Rankin's YouTube video chronicling her experimental use of Twitter as a learning tool in her University of Texas at Dallas history course as well as by Cole Camplese's use of Twitter in his educational technology courses.[1] Filgo, who thought Twitter could provide her with a unique opportunity to be an embedded librarian in a content area course, approached Dr. Campbell, who was the director of Baylor's Academy for Teaching and Learning, with the idea. Campbell wanted his students to construct and experience a **personal cyberinfrastructure**, a learning environment in which they would "acquire crucial technical skills for their digital lives but also would engage in work that provides richly teachable moments ranging from multimodal writing to information science, knowledge management, bibliographic instruction, and social networking. Fascinating and important innovations would emerge as students are able to shape their own cognition, learning, expression, and reflection in a digital age, in a digital medium. Students would frame, curate, share, and direct their own 'engagement streams' throughout the learning environment."[2]

The class blog (see figure 6) was the virtual centerpiece for students in the new media studies course. Because the course blog included RSS feeds for the course hashtag Tweets, student blogs, the course bookmarks via Delicious, and Filgo's course librarian blog, everyone was able to easily access each other's content and interact with that content in a variety of virtual media and applications like Google Reader and TweetDeck to organize and follow the information streams.

Embedded Instruction and Help through Twitter

Because students were using Twitter as a backchannel for class conversation during face-to-face meetings, Filgo needed a way to organize the Twitter communications as she followed and interacted with the class virtually from her office. Filgo's organizational strategy was to create groups that she could easily monitor and follow in TweetDeck, a free application that allows users to organize streams of Twitter users and hashtags. TweetChat is another tool one can use to track and participate in a specific hashtag discussion.

Figure 6
"From Memex to YouTube" Fall 2010 Course Blog

Filgo created groups for course hashtags #nmsf09 and #nms_f10; she also created a group with the usernames of each class member.

TweetDeck
www.tweetdeck.com

TweetChat
http://tweetchat.com

Since students were not accustomed to a librarian being an instructional partner in their college coursework, Campbell would remind students at the beginning of the class of Filgo's virtual presence; this opening Twitter greeting was also a cue to Filgo that discussion was beginning so that she was prepared and focused on interacting with students through the virtual discussion. Filgo's professional skills in multitasking and search strategies were sharpened since she had to be ready to respond to a comment or inquiry on a moment's notice on any topic that came up during the class conversation. How did Filgo contribute to these Twitter conversations? Her interactions took many forms, including providing

- resources related to the author the class was reading or discussing, including articles from the library's databases, *Wikipedia* articles, and YouTube videos
- titles of related books or readings relevant to a topic or author of study
- resources related to comments Tweeted by students that might have seemed off topic but that Filgo tried to relate back to the main class conversation

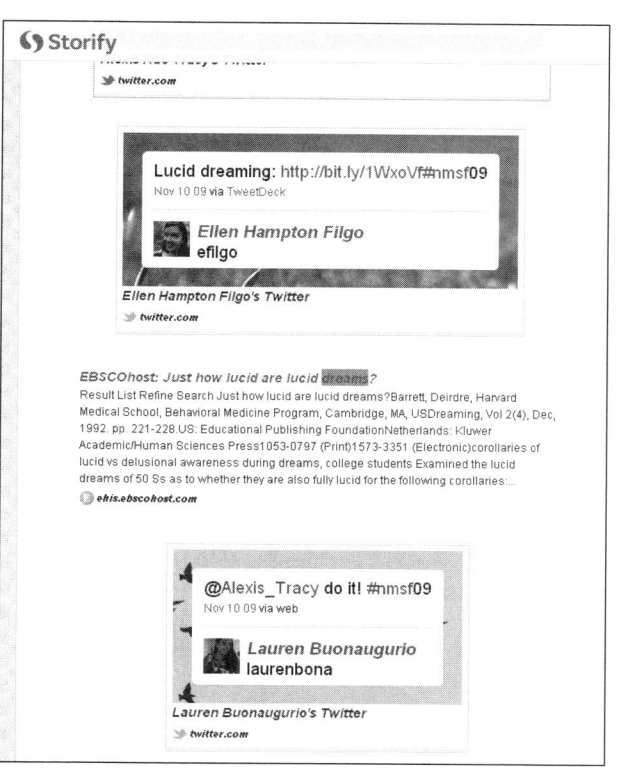

Figure 7
Librarian Jazz on Storify

Filgo came to conceptualize this interaction as **Librarian Jazz** (see figure 7). In reflecting on her experiences, Filgo mused, "The class discussion was the music and the melody was happening in another classroom across campus. Every once in a while, the students would throw out a note or two, or a stray chord, which I would pick up through Twitter. I had to improvise, tossing out my own chords and riffs back into the Twitter stream, hoping that they would add to the music being made."[3] One example of this Librarian Jazz was a class discussion about the Clifford D. Simak short science fiction story "The Immigrant." Filgo had not had an opportunity to read the story prior to the class discussion and experienced difficulty inferring the key ideas about the work from the Twitter conversation, so she did some research on the author; she discovered a collection of Simak's papers through the University of Minnesota. She decided to Tweet the link to the collection as well as a link to the covers of *Astounding Science Fiction* in which "The Immigrant" was published in 1954. Within a few minutes, a student sent a direct message to Filgo wanting to know if she could find any similar articles and resources for another 1950s science fiction writer, Rilke; Filgo responded by starting a new search and within a few minutes, she was able to provide links to the requested materials to a very appreciate student. While the author material requested by the student was not directly linked to the course discussion that particular day, Filgo's willingness to provide assistance in an immediate and personal manner made an impression and helped to create a rapport between librarian and student while showing the power of improvised search and how one topic can lead to an interest in another.

In another case of improvisation and meeting learners at their point of need, Filgo helped a student discover a career pathway. After watching a clip from the film *Waking Life,* the class was engaging in a discussion about the concept of lucid dreaming; while Filgo was Tweeting resources for this concept, the class began discussing the term *oneirology,* the scientific study of dreams. After a student expressed an interest in exploring oneirology as a career, Filgo searched the library's card catalog and Tweeted information about a three-volume work on the emerging science of the study of dreams. The student, who immediately Tweeted, "I want that book!" was so delighted with the immediate response from Filgo that she nearly jumped out of her chair with excitement. Additionally, the assistance Filgo provided helped cultivate a relationship with this student that would go beyond this particular course; the student sought Filgo's help in subsequent semesters for research projects in other courses.

You can see the curated content of these instances of Librarian Jazz on Filgo's Storify account.

Librarian Jazz on Storify
http://storify.com/efilgo/librarian-jazz

Blogs as a Medium for Help and Student Interaction

Blogs provided Filgo another medium for following the progress of student thinking and content creation. Filgo, who subscribed to a master RSS feed that Campbell had created for all student blog feeds, kept up with student posts through Google Reader. When appropriate, Filgo would provide feedback, commentary, and helpful resources in response to student posts. This medium of interaction took on even greater significance as students began blogging more about the final research projects; consequently, Filgo was able to provide more feedback on blog posts and intervention for students who had questions or who were struggling as part of the formative assessment process. Because she was able to interact with students through the blogs in a one-on-one manner, Filgo was able to help students through the entire research process, which was especially important as students were exploring possible research topics and formulating their strategies for accessing information sources and organizing

Figure 8
Twitter Conversations for Learning Between Ellen Hampton Filgo and Students

their findings for their projects. This early and regular intervention resulted in research projects that were of higher quality and less stressful for students since they were receiving personalized and regular feedback from Filgo.

Reflections on Student Learning and Partnerships for Learning

Students came to regard Filgo as the "magical librarian" or "guardian librarian" because of her expertise in providing resources in such a spontaneous and timely manner through the Twitter backchannel and her virtual assistance through their learning blogs (see figure 9). In an informal postcourse survey, students shared extremely positive feedback about having an embedded librarian in their course. According to Filgo, one student remarked, "The librarian's participation was, I think, a critical part of the class because the librarian was able to provide outside resources and spend time looking for those resources that proved relevant to the class, a task which students would be unlikely to do at all, much less during a class."[4]

In addition, students indicated they felt their level of expertise about library resources and search skills improved as a result of Filgo's role as an instructional

Figure 9
Ellen Hampton Filgo Poster Session, "The Hashtag Librarian," ACRL 2011 (used with permission)

partner in the course. Filgo also found that her interaction with students increased outside of class, including an increase in the number of students booking appointment for reference help; many students also sought additional virtual help for the course assignments as well as research project challenges in other courses through e-mail, Twitter, and Facebook. These transactional learning experiences cultivated a sense of trust, and the relationship between the librarian and students transcended just one semester; students regarded Filgo as more than a librarian—they came to see her as a guide, a learning coach, and a teacher who cared about their work and who was genuinely happy to provide assistance and help develop their skills. Because she was naturally integrated into the course as an essential resource, her assistance and instruction were more authentic for students' learning experiences.

Best Practices and Suggestions for Implementation

The two-year partnership for learning between Filgo and Campbell provided them with insights into best steps and practices for establishing this type of embedded instruction from librarians into content area courses:

- The librarian should attend at least one initial class meeting to help students put a face with the librarian's name. Even one face-to-face meeting with students can help establish a bridge in the relationship between the physical class meetings and the librarian's virtual participation. Additional periodic visits during the semester can also enhance the relationship-building process in the learning community.
- Embedded librarianship is a time-intensive endeavor, so plan your schedule thoughtfully. For this particular course, Filgo was committed to participating virtually twice during the week for a total of three hours a week; in addition, she spent time outside of class on reading student Tweets, blog posts, e-mails, and Facebook messages, as well as on one-on-one reference sessions.
- Create and use a course hashtag to focus students' Tweets around a class identity and to provide a common hashtag for organizing the virtual conversations for learning.
- Archive your course Tweets since Twitter's search ability is limited. TwapperKeeper was a popular choice for many, but it was recently purchased by Hootsuite; it is not clear at this time if or how Hootsuite will support the archiving of Tweets.
- Consider media for curating all course social media streams and conversations for learning. Tools like Storify and Summify can pull in feeds from your course social media networks.

Storify
http://storify.com

Summify
www.summify.com

- Use a URL shortener that provides statistics on the number of click-throughs to evaluate the effectiveness and use of librarian-Tweeted resources by participants. Bitly and Google's URL shortener are two possible choices.

Bitly
http://bitly.com

Google URL shortener
http:/goo.gl

- Choose your partnerships wisely—teachers who are willing to share the control of content and instructional design and to take risks as instructors and learners themselves are the best candidates for establishing this type of teaching partnership. Filgo believes that "what is important is an understanding that the professor and the students can use new technologies to work and learn together."[5]
- Focus on creating connections with students and the learning community so that you can build a sense of trust and show students you are fully invested in enhancing their learning experiences.

Conclusion

Filgo's experiences represent the possibilities for a librarian to become meaningfully embedded in the lives of students and to enrich the learning experiences in content area courses. Rather than waiting for students to come to us, these forms of embedded librarianship allow librarians to create conversations for learning in the context of real-world information-seeking tasks. By modeling effective information and digital literacy skills and strategies on a regular basis as part of a class discussion and through one-on-one personal interactions, librarians can elevate their roles as teacher and instructional partner with faculty so that students gain confidence not only in themselves as learners but also in librarians as real people who can provide meaningful help throughout the student's academic experience.

Notes

1. Monica Rankin and Kim Smith, "The Twitter Experiment: Twitter in the Classroom," video, YouTube, May 2, 2009, accessed Dec. 29, 2011, www.youtube.com/watch?v=6WPVWDkF7U8. Cole Camplese, "Connections," http://colecamplese.typepad.com/my_blog/2008/05/connections.html.
2. Gardner Campbell, "A Personal Cyberinfrastructure." *EDUCAUSE Review* 44, no. 5 (Sept./Oct. 2009): 58–59, accessed Dec. 5, 2011, www.educause.edu/EDUCAUSE+Review/EDUCAUSEReviewMagazineVolume44/APersonalCyberinfrastructure/178431.
3. Ellen Hampton Filgo, "Hashtag Librarian: Embedded in a Class via Twitter and Blogs," EllenFilgo.net, 2011, accessed Dec. 5, 2011, www.ellenfilgo.net/hashtag-librarian.
4. Ibid.
5. Ibid.

Chapter 5

Embedded Librarianship in a High School Library
Cultivating Student Participatory Literacy and Personal Learning Environments

Buffy J. Hamilton

Abstract

This case study chronicles the learning experiences of three cohorts of tenth-grade students taking an honors literature/composition course (also known as Media 21) cotaught by high school librarian Buffy Hamilton and English teacher Susan Lester between August 2009 and the present. This class, which takes an inquiry stance on information, digital, and participatory literacy, has provided students a learning environment in which Hamilton is intensely involved in the instructional design, teaching, and assessment of student learning for approximately 75 percent of the academic year. Hamilton shares how she utilized teaching technologies to teach key processes and skills to cultivate network and information attention and to provide students feedback and assistance through virtual cloud computing applications.

Introduction

Librarians function as sponsors of literacy1 by promoting traditional forms of information literacy—as well as new literacies—to encourage many voices of discourse and representations of information. To embed information literacy as an essential standard in every subject area, librarians must collaborate with subject-area teachers to foster an inquiry-based approach that dovetails perfectly with the use of social networks and new media as part of students' personal learning networks and the syntheses of information gleaned from a diverse range of these information sources. By responding to the changes that are occurring in today's information culture, librarians can facilitate learning experiences that situate information literacy as a fundamental literacy shaped by today's society, culture, and ever-evolving technologies and provide students with a sense of agency by teaching them strategies and tools for harnessing a dizzying array of information streams.

Participatory librarianship positions librarians as agents of change in their learning communities. Rooted in conversation theory, participatory librarianship suggests that if people must engage in some form of conversation to acquire knowledge and if librarians are in the knowledge business, then librarians should be in the conversation business. All efforts to engage patrons and plan library programming should go back to the essential question "How does this decision impact and create a conversation for learning?"[2] Librarians seek to create such conversations providing an information-rich environment with multiple points of access to the information.[3]

Consequently, librarians should consider how to facilitate these conversations about information literacy with learners through the use of social media and cloud computing. Helping students create their own **personal learning environments** and information dashboards allows them to engage in these conversations for learning with themselves as well as with peers within and outside the classroom. Such learning tools are critical in teaching students how to navigate today's information landscape and to initiate and sustain their own conversations for learning.

What is a personal learning environment (PLE)? PLEs are "systems that help learners take control of and manage their own learning. This includes providing support for learners to set their own learning goals, manage their learning; managing both content and process, and communicate with others in the process of learning."[4]

In today's mashup world of information, a plethora of resources are available via the Internet, including podcasts, blogs, social bookmarks, social networks, videos and video streaming, wikis, and RSS feeds through a favorite feed aggregator. The premise behind participatory tools used to build these information dashboards and personal learning environments is to model ethical and informed information-seeking behavior for our students. Students learn how to connect with other learners and entities to build knowledge and solve information-search problems.[5] Information literacy instruction must include helping students learn to pick and evaluate the best resources for their personal learning environments from print, subscriptions, and emerging forms of authoritative information via social media streams.

Collaborative Seeds

Creekview High School librarian Buffy Hamilton and English teacher Susan Lester, have collaborated together as coteachers of tenth-grade honors world literature/composition for nearly three years to create a learning environment in which Hamilton was embedded as an instructor. These sections of sophomore English courses, also known as Media 21, are rooted in connectivism, inquiry, and participatory literacy and emphasize students creating their own research dashboards and portals. The course also teaches students to craft personal learning environments to help them develop nodes in their network of resources for learning and to evaluate a diverse offering of information sources more critically.

The collaborative process began in March 2009. Hamilton approached Lester with an idea for a collaborative project grounded in connectivism and participatory librarianship. For her Media 21 Capstone project,[6] Hamilton wanted to create a nine-to-twelve-week-long learning experience that would help students learn how to use social media and cloud computing for learning and as a means of cultivating a personal learning network. In addition, Hamilton wanted students to engage in learning through collective knowledge building and inquiry. After Hamilton shared with Lester the resources and research she had collected to support this vision of learning, Lester agreed to take a leap of faith and join Hamilton on this journey of teaching and learning. Together, the two outlined content-based and information literacy performance standards they wanted students to master; they also collaborated to draft a list of learning activities and tools they wanted to implement, as well as a master list of materials.

Google Sites and Wordpress

Over the last three years, Hamilton has utilized a variety of virtual tools for supporting student learning. Hamilton has used Google Sites and Wordpress as media for providing students access to course materials and a daily learning agenda. These course websites reflect the instructional planning and course content creation between Hamilton and Lester as they codesign and share the responsibility of creating instructional handouts, assessment rubrics, and the daily calendar of learning activities and resources, but Hamilton is responsible for organizing and posting the content. During the 2009–10 and 2010–11 academic years, Hamilton utilized Google Sites since students were learning how to use that tool for creating their learning portfolios, but she primarily used it as a medium for hosting course content since students could subscribe to daily updates via RSS. In the fall of the 2011–12 year, she decided to use Wordpress.com (see figure 10) as the host of the course agenda and daily class materials since it provided options for both RSS and e-mail updates to students. In addition, Wordpress is the host of the course blog and the platform for student blogging, so it provided a familiar interface for students. In addition, Hamilton used research guides she created in LibGuides as a medium for igniting conversations about information literacy skills and digital literacy skills with students.

Media 21 LibGuides
www.theunquietlibrary.libguides.com/media21

Wordpress has also been the platform for student blogging and a space for students to reflect on their research and learning processes. Not only has blogging provided students an opportunity for metacognition, but it has provided a virtual means for Hamilton to provide formative assessment and suggestions for students to help them deal with their research challenges in a personal and individualized manner. While she originally used Netvibes to follow student blog entries via RSS feed, she eventually used Google Reader to

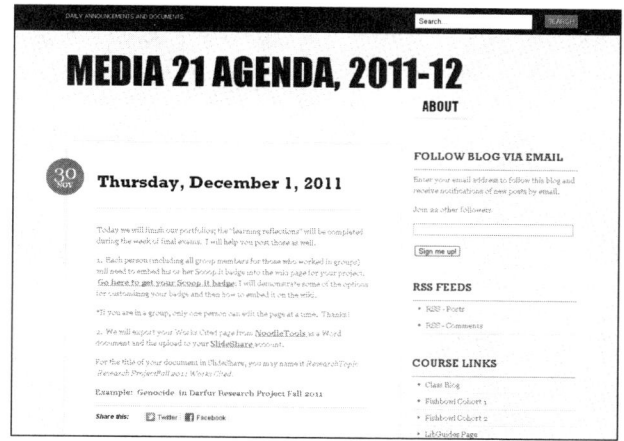

Figure 10
Media 21 class learning agenda on Wordpress

access and interact with student blog posts because it provided her a faster and more accessible way of dealing with up to 65 individual student blogs.

Symbaloo

Symbaloo is another medium for instructional support that Hamilton has maintained with students (see figure 11). Through Symbaloo, librarians can create webmixes—tabs or pages with tiles containing web links to any information source or RSS feed. Because these webmixes can be published and shared with other Symbaloo users, Hamilton decided to utilize Symbaloo as an information dashboard that would provide students with a jumping off point each day in class to easily access all course resources in one place. This dashboard was easy to navigate and could exist with student-created mixes in their own Symbaloo accounts. Not only did the use of Symbaloo allow Hamilton to broadcast resource updates directly to students' individual Symbaloo accounts, but it also served as a model of an information dashboard for students as they worked to craft their own research guides on topics they were researching in a unit on the issues and challenges facing veterans who served in Afghanistan and Iraq. Resources in the course webmix created by Hamilton have included

- links to research databases provided by the library as well as by GALILEO, Georgia's state virtual library
- recommended search engines like SweetSearch and NewsTrust
- course virtual spaces for learning, including the class wiki, class blog, LibGuide pages for units of research, the course daily agenda, and links to student learning portfolios
- sources for copyright-friendly images

Figure 11
Media 21 Symbaloo account

- virtual tools for student learning, including Evernote, Scoop.it, and Google Docs
- the library OPAC
- NoodleTools for citation and electronic notetaking
- tutorial videos
- course surveys conducted through SurveyMonkey and Google Forms

Wikis

Hamilton has also utilized wikis for interacting with students and providing support for student learning. Initially, she used Wetpaint as a space for students to share and discuss articles and to provide commentary on student discussion threads, but after one semester, she and Lester decided to use the blog for discussions and to harness the use of wikis for students building and sharing content. As the facilitator of the class wiki, Hamilton assisted students in learning how to use Wikispaces to create project pages and embed original content they were creating to represent key insights and learning artifacts of their research process. These class wikis have included

- multigenre research projects that included a combination of traditional texts that students wrote collaboratively in Google Docs and alternate genres of "writing" such as videos, artwork, two-voice poems, character and event recipes, music playlists, word clouds, and skits
- the discussion feature available for each page in the wiki utilized by students to provide constructive peer review and feedback

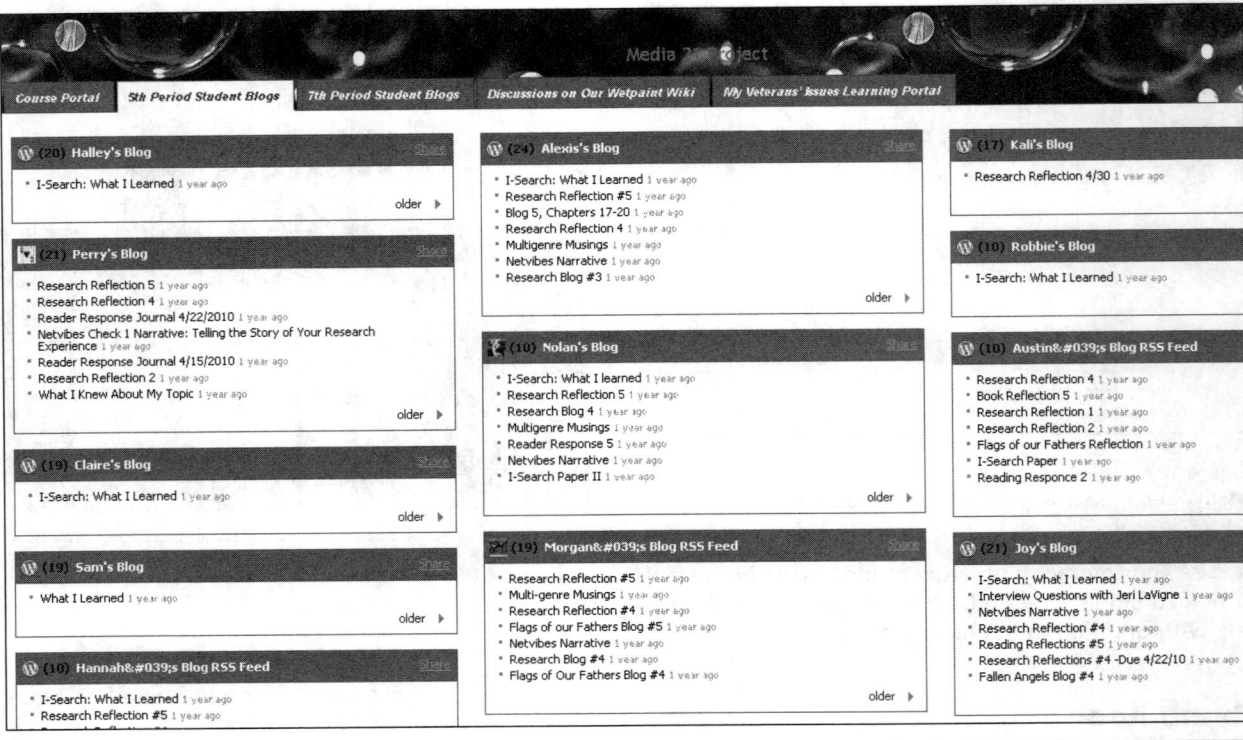

Figure 12
Netvibes Media 21 course portal

- incorporation of digital texts that have combined embedded multimedia juxtaposed traditional research writing
- learning portfolios that have included embedded research design proposals, digital texts in Prezi or VoiceThread format, embedded Works Cited pages, embedded badges for Scoop.it research magazines, and RSS feeds for published Evernote research notebooks and their embedded "presentation Zen" style slidedecks

Netvibes

Hamilton has also utilized Netvibes as a way of providing students a course hub where they could easily follow the RSS feeds of course content (the class daily agenda, course bookmark feeds, and RSS feeds of each student learning blog, as well as the course blog) and access and interact with these media. In addition, Netvibes has provided students with a way to digitally showcase their information sources, tools for learning and research, and learning artifacts; in other words, Netvibes has served as a hub for students to create a digital narrative of all aspects of their research and learning processes (see figure 12). The purpose of incorporating Netvibes as a learning tool was to give students a means of creating an information dashboard for organizing all of their information sources (RSS feeds from informational or peer blogs, online news sources, saved database searches, widgets for databases, books or other print materials from Google Books, informational videos, and RSS feeds for posts and comments from their individual learning blogs). This decision was inspired by Howard Rheingold's concept of **infotention** and his assertion that "Knowing how to put together intelligence dashboards, news radars, and information filters from online tools like persistent search and RSS is the external technical component of information literacy. Knowing what to pay attention to is a cognitive skill that steers and focuses the technical knowledge of how to find information worth your attention."[7]

Many students liked Netvibe's extensive gallery of widgets they could use in addition to the diverse range of themes for a custom look and feel; several students also commented that they found it easy to add content and embed more types of Web code to showcase their learning tools and artifacts. Students also enjoyed using the news widgets available in Netvibes for discovering news articles on their research topic. While students were provided with a list of required elements for their Netvibes information portals/learning dashboards, they also had flexibility and creative license in choosing additional content to incorporate and paint a digital story of their research process. By creating these information dashboards, students could easily access their information sources and were cultivating their own information fluency by constructing individualized research guides for their topics. Netvibes also made it easy for both Hamilton and the students to follow each student's blog and to regularly comment and interact with each other through commenting on their learning blogs hosted in Wordpress.

NoodleBib

Hamilton wanted to embed herself in virtual student learning spaces not just to provide resources and virtual help, but also to utilize these spaces as a way of providing formative assessment to both the students and Lester, her coteacher. One way Hamilton engaged in meaningful formative assessment was through the NoodleBib shared assignment dropbox feature that is part of the NoodleTools suite, a comprehensive citation management package subscription provided by Hamilton's district to every school. NoodleBib's dropbox features allow Hamilton to virtually evaluate bibliographies in progress and electronic notecards (see figure 13). The assignment dropbox has allowed Hamilton to be successful in engaging in formative assessment and has enabled her

- to gain insights into the selection of information sources by students and to help students identify sources they may have overlooked that could inform their research
- to help students identify and understand the mistakes they've made in the citation process and work with them to correct the entries
- to see what students are doing really well with their notetaking skills and provide positive feedback while identifying areas of weakness and then engaging in a conversation for learning with the student by sharing strategies for tackling those "challenge" areas

Hamilton's roles in facilitating these formative assessments included

- setting up the shared assignment dropboxes
- teaching students how to share an assignment and confirming she had received the assignments from each group
- taking the time to evaluate each group's bibliographic entries and notecards while providing feedback
- keeping a spreadsheet of general notes for each group's work and noting patterns in what students were doing well and common problems she saw in student work

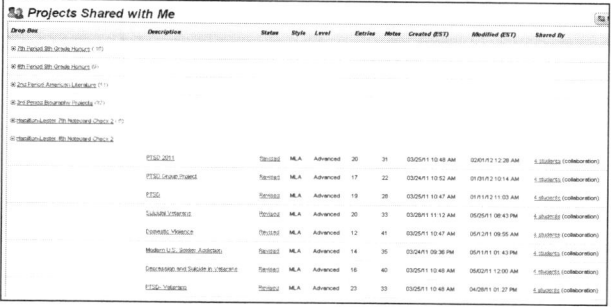

Figure 13
NoodleTools dropbox

- sharing her findings and notes with Lester, which enabled the two of them to work together with small groups during the face-to-face class meetings to address challenges Hamilton had identified, and in addition, enlisting the assistance of students who were demonstrating specific skills in an exemplary manner to help peers on an "as needed" basis

Hamilton loved how easy it was to evaluate bibliographic individual entries and the accompanying notecards for each source cited in one screen. This virtual space was an essential tool in providing students with feedback and igniting conversations about information sources.

Scoop.it and Curation

In the fall of 2011, Hamilton introduced Scoop.it (see figure 14) to the sophomores as a tool for curating and collecting resources on their research topic. Scoop.it is a free online tool that allows users to aggregate content from any source—the open Web or a database—and publish those resources in a website that looks like a beautiful visual magazine. As students created their "magazines" for their research topics and shared them with Hamilton, she followed their topics through her Scoop.it dashboard. Each day, Hamilton received a summary via e-mail of new activity on all the topics she followed; through this update, she could quickly see what sources students were exploring and collecting for their research. A bonus of the Follow feature is that students can easily follow the research of their classmates or experts outside the classroom who are curating resources on their research topics. Scoop.it also enables students to crosspost content to other potential learning, sharing, and reflection spaces, such as Facebook, Tumblr, Wordpress, and Twitter. In addition, as she viewed student topic magazines, Hamilton could easily suggest additional resources or offer commentary as needed on a source in a student's topic magazine.

Reflections and Conclusions

What factors are conducive to this kind of collaborative partnership between a librarian and an academic instructor? First, the librarian and teacher shared similar philosophies about teaching and learning. Without this shared vision of learning goals, the trust needed to cultivate this partnership would not have been possible. Another important element in this case study was the teacher's willingness to open up the possibilities of the physical and virtual spaces of the classroom. The class, which met primarily in the library, was able to establish a sense of community fairly quickly because of the collaborative and transparent nature of the course; the classroom was also open 24/7 because the students, librarian, and classroom teacher were able to communicate virtually after class hours through blogs, wikis, and e-mail.

Another important factor in this case study was the teacher's willingness to share ownership of content, pedagogy, and assessment practices that helped establish the librarian as a true coteacher of the course. Students recognized quickly that the librarian was not there just to provide ancillary support or just to teach information literacy skills, but that both Hamilton and Lester were facilitators of the learning activities and practices. One other essential ingredient for the success of this model has been Hamilton and Lester's willingness to focus on conversations about the concept of authority with students and to engage in inquiry about how and why information sources are appropriate for information-seeking tasks.

Based on this experience of being embedded in a class through face-to-face time as well as virtual spaces, Hamilton can't help but wonder how much more seamless and authentic research, content creation, and evaluation of information could be if more school librarians were embedded in a team of classroom teachers by grade level or discipline. The Media 21 embedded librarian model provides a glimpse of how school librarians can help teachers, students, and school librarians engage in conversations about multiple forms of literacy and consequently position information literacy as an essential literacy integrated into content area instruction. Research, information seeking and evaluation, and creation of content would no longer be isolated activities students engaged in once or twice or year, but instead, a regular learning experience. Hamilton hopes that Media 21 will inspire school districts to reconsider the current model of the solitary librarianship that creates an imbalance of staffing that is in direct conflict with the model of twenty-first-century classrooms that value learning focused on collective intelligence and collaborative knowledge building as a community of learners and instead forge a new model in which additional school librarians will be integrated into the faculty to help create these rich kinds of learning experiences for teachers and students.

Figure 14
Scoop.it

Notes

1. Deborah Brandt, *Literacy in American Lives* (New York: Cambridge University Press, 2001), 19.
2. The Information Institute of Syracuse, "Introduction," The Participatory Librarianship Starter Kit," accessed Jan. 22, 2009, http://quartz.syr.edu/rdlankes/intro.php.
3. R. David Lankes, "Welcome," video, The Atlas of New Librarianship Companion Website, Institute of Museum and Library Services, accessed Dec. 19, 2011, www.newlibrarianship.org/wordpress. R. David Lankes, "Participatory Librarianship," video, YouTube, July 3, 2007, accessed Dec. 11, 2011, www.youtube.com/watch?v=7TyuVJ4vENo.
4. Wikipedia, s.v. "Personal learning environment," last modified Dec. 9, 2011, accessed Dec. 11, 2011, http://en.wikipedia.org/wiki/Personal_learning_environment.
5. Wendy Drexler, "Networked Student," video, YouTube, Nov. 26, 2008, accessed Dec. 11, 2011, www.youtube.com/watch?v=XwM4ieFOotA.
6. Please see Cherokee County [Georgia] School District, "Media21 Endorsement Program," accessed Dec. 29, 2011, http://portal.cherokee.k12.ga.us/departments/technology/media/default.aspx.
7. Howard Rheingold, "Mindful Infotention: Dashboards, Radars, Filters," Howard Rheingold: Online Instigator (blog), SFGate website, Sept. 1, 2009, accessed Dec. 29, 2011, http://blog.sfgate.com/rheingold/2009/09/01/mindful-infotention-dashboards-radars-filters.

Chapter 6

Conclusion

Best Tools and Practices

Buffy J. Hamilton

Abstract

This chapter identifies resources for growing one's knowledge, best practices, instructional strategies, and technology toolkit for embedded librarians.

Embedded librarianship is a model that embodies many possibilities for disrupting stereotypes of a library as a warehouse of books rather than a dynamic commonplace site where learning and people shape the narrative of the library experience for a learning community, whether it be a school, academic, or public library. By considering how social media, cloud computing, and other emerging technologies can be used to support the mission of "improving society through facilitating knowledge creation in their communities,"[1] librarians can utilize these technologies to engage patrons, build relationships, and compose a new story of librarianship with their learning communities.

Embedded Librarianship for Creating Enchantment

These technologies also bolster librarians' efforts to foster **enchantment**, "the process of delighting people with a product, service, and organization of idea. The outcome of enchantment is voluntary and long-lasting support that is mutually beneficial."[2] By building relationships with individuals or groups through embedded librarianship, we can establish the three principles of enchantment: likability, trustworthiness, and a fantastic product or service.[3] The technologies featured in each of these case studies exemplify how librarians can utilize virtual tools for getting to know the community members who are being served in the partnership for learning; social media and cloud computing tools help librarians to go beyond surface relationships with patrons and allow us to better know and understand the needs, passions, and wishes of patrons and to know them as humans—what they care about, what troubles them, and what stories of learning they have to share and construct. By providing positive learning experiences through face-to-face interactions and the use of virtual tools and technologies, librarians create powerful learning experiences for patrons that form positive memories and attachment to the library as a node in one's personal learning environment for multiple information-seeking needs.

Embedded librarianship ultimately focuses on the human element of library, and the use of technology to honor and privilege the relationships that libraries can nurture through embedded librarianship provides points of transformation for making the library more relevant and meaningful. These technologies also provide a more authentic context for dialogic practice in which the transactions with the members of a learning community served through embedded librarianship informs our practice and principles of library programming and services.

Using Virtual Tools and Practices in Embedded Librarianship to Address Digital and Participation Divides

The case studies in this report represent how virtual tools and practices enhance the embedded librarian's efforts to address the digital divide and close the participation gap in learning communities. By modeling the use of these technologies in a relevant way that is part of a larger effort to teach others how to harness the powers of these tools for learning, librarians can more effectively teach information skills and processes as they address the "inequalities in the networked world . . . the lack of digital and media literacies; critical thinking and communication skills in order to navigate and evaluate data online; an information and knowledge gap; and collaboration and participatory inequalities"[4] The collaborative nature of embedded librarianship, particularly when supported through the use of social media and cloud computing, reflects the findings of Danica Radovanovic's forthcoming dissertation research that shows "collaboration possibilities using the Internet and social media services present one of the communication practices for overcoming inequalities in e-skills, twenty-first century literacies and communication, and foster better collaboration and participation."[5] In other words, the technologies are not enough in and of themselves to closes these gaps, but instead, collaborative human partnerships are needed to provide people context and learning spaces for harnessing the participatory power of these technologies and to grow their digital and information literacy skills.

Resources for Learning about Teaching, Learning, and Technology

As librarians, we are always looking for resources to add to our own personal learning environment to provide inspiration and ideas for ways to incorporate technology as a medium for teaching and learning in a variety of settings that can be applied to our own work as embedded librarians. Below is a listing of my favorite resources for learning how others are using emerging technologies to create meaningful learning experiences. While not every resource is specifically about embedded librarianship, they provide examples and best practices in other learning environments that can be applied to your own situation. Each resource includes the title, URL, and quotations from the official description from the site's About page. I also invite you to follow my curated resources on embedded librarianship and learning at www.scoop.it/t/embedded-librarianship.

DMLcentral (Digital Media Central) Digital Media and Learning: The Power of Participation
http://dmlcentral.net
DMLcentral is a "collaborative blog" curating a "collection of free and open resources produced by the Digital Media and Learning Research Hub," a group "dedicated to analyzing and interpreting the impact of the Internet and digital media on education, civic engagement, and youth."

Mind/Shift
http://mindshift.kqed.org
MindShift explores how technology is transforming the future of learning now. Curated by journalist Tina Barseghian, the site covers "cultural and technology trends, groundbreaking research, education policy, and more."

Digital Ethnography @Kansas State University
http://mediatedcultures.net/ksudigg
Digital Ethnography is "a Kansas State University working group led by Dr. Michael Wesch dedicated to exploring and extending the possibilities of digital ethnography."

School Library Monthly Blog
http://blog.schoollibrarymedia.com
"The mission of the *SLM* blog is to extend the magazine into the digital realm and model the thoughtful Web 2.0 engagement that we advocate for in print. With weekly updates, it is a digital column that can respond nimbly to current events, model self-reflection, and inspire our readers to take thoughtful action. . . . Our blogger is Kristin Fontichiaro, a clinical assistant professor and coordinator of the school library media program at the University of Michigan School of Information."

ProfHacker @ The Chronicle of Higher Education
http://chronicle.com/blogs/profhacker
Monday through Friday, *ProfHacker* delivers "tips, tutorials, and commentary on pedagogy, productivity, and technology in higher education."

Info-mational
http://infomational.wordpress.com
Info-mational is the blog of Char Booth, "Instruction Services Manager & E-Learning Librarian at the Claremont Colleges Library." She writes about "instructional design and pedagogy, emerging technology development, collaboration and outreach, user assessment, teaching effectiveness, and learning technologies."

Wired Campus @ The Chronicle of Higher Education
http://chronicle.com/blogs/wiredcampus
The Wired Campus provides "the latest news on tech and education" with a focus on libraries, publishing, research, student life, teaching, and software.

Powerful Learning Practice Blog
http://plpnetwork.com/blog
Powerful Learning Practice Blog is provided by a learning community dedicated to "enabling thousands of educators around the country to experience the transformative power of the social Web: Face-to-face in their own schools, exchanging ideas through a community of inquiry, and in re-envisioning their own personal learning practice."

HASTAC
http://hastac.org

"HASTAC ('haystack') is a network of individuals and institutions inspired by the possibilities that new technologies offer us for shaping how we learn, teach, communicate, create, and organize our local and global communities. We are motivated by the conviction that the digital era provides rich opportunities for informal and formal learning and for collaborative, networked research that extends across traditional disciplines, across the boundaries of academe and community, across the 'two cultures' of humanism and technology, across the divide of thinking versus making, and across social strata and national borders."

The New Media Consortium
http://www.nmc.org

"The NMC (New Media Consortium) is an international community of experts in educational technology—from the practitioners who work with new technologies on campuses every day; to the visionaries who are shaping the future of learning at think tanks, labs, and research centers; to its staff and board of directors; to the advisory boards and others helping the NMC conduct cutting edge research."

PBS MediaShift
http://www.pbs.org/mediashift

"MediaShift tracks how new media—from weblogs to podcasts to citizen journalism—are changing society and culture."

Howard Rheingold
www.rheingold.com

Rheingold.com is the home page of scholar, teacher, and info-attention evangelist Howard Rheingold. It has links to his videos, articles, syllabi, and other spaces for content creation and sharing.

The Atlas of New Librarianship Companion Website
www.newlibrarianship.org/wordpress

This website is not just a companion to the book but also a classroom and participatory space for those interested in learning about new librarianship. "The site is the access; the Atlas, videos, and short courses constitute the base knowledge of new librarianship; integration with Facebook and other social media tools provide an open environment; and we'll do our best to motivate you."

Learning and Laptops
http://learningandlaptops.blogspot.com

Learning and Laptops is a collaborative blog from the faculty of Arapahoe High School focusing on learning and the chronicles of the integration of technology into high school classrooms and the impact on learning resulting from these shifts.

Teach Web
http://teachweb2.blogspot.com

Teach Web is Dr. Wendy Drexler's blog about personal learning environments and learner empowerment.

Confessions of an Aca-Fan: The Official Weblog of Henry Jenkins
http://henryjenkins.org/index.html

Confessions of an Aca-Fan is the blog where, as Jenkins says, "I share my thoughts about many contemporary developments and publish my works in progress. It is also a space where I showcase the work of my students at MIT and now at USC and give you a glimpse into the world where I live and work." Jenkins also "spotlight[s] interesting work in the field of media studies which may be relevant to a readership that includes not only academics but also journalists, educators, industry insiders, policy makers, fans and gamers."

The Ubiquitous Librarian
http://chronicle.com/blognetwork/theubiquitouslibrarian

"*The Ubiquitous Librarian* is the blog of Brian Mathews, Associate Dean for Learning & Outreach at the Virginia Tech University Libraries. His goal is to develop user-sensitive libraries that foster a culture of creativity, productivity, and scholarship."

EllenFilgo.net: My Information Sandbox
www.ellenfilgo.net

EllenFilgo.net is the thinking space of Ellen Hampton Filgo, E-Learning Librarian in the Reference and Instruction Department of Baylor University Libraries, where she contemplates "ways that new generations of students are using the Internet and how that can be connected with the online resources the library provides."

Virtualpolitik
www.virtualpolitik.blogspot.com

Virtualpolitik, the blog of Liz Losh, is "about digital rhetoric that asks the burning questions about electronic bureaucracy and institutional subversion on the Internet."

ACRL (Association of College and Research Libraries)
College and Research Libraries News
http://crln.acrl.org

"Established in 1966, *College & Research Libraries News* (*C&RL News*) provides articles on the latest trends and practices affecting academic and research libraries and serves as the official newsmagazine and publication of record of ACRL."

Notes

1. R. David Lankes, "Welcome," video, *The Atlas of New Librarianship* Companion Website, Institute

of Museum and Library Services, accessed Dec. 19, 2011, www.newlibrarianship.org/wordpress.
2. Guy Kawasaki, *Enchantment: The Art of Changing Hearts, Minds, and Actions* (New York: Portfolio/Penguin, 2011), introduction.
3. Ibid.
4. Danica Radovanovic, "Digital Divide and Social Media: Connectivity Doesn't End the Digital Divide, Skills Do," Guest Blog, *Scientific American* website, Dec. 14, 2011, accessed Dec. 19, 2011, http://blogs.scientificamerican.com/guest-blog/2011/12/14/digital-divide-and-social-media-connectivity-doesnt-end-the-digital-divide-skills-do.
5. Ibid.

Notes

Library Technology Reports Respond to Your Library's Digital Dilemmas

Eight times per year, *Library Technology Reports* (*LTR*) provides library professionals with insightful elucidation, covering the technology and technological issues the library world grapples with on a daily basis in the information age.

	Library Technology Reports 2012, Vol. 48
January 48:1	**Bridging the Digital Divide with Mobile Services** by Andomeda Yelton
February/ March 48:2	**Embedded Librarianship: Tools and Practices** by Buffy J. Hamilton
April 48:3	**Gadgets and Gizmos: Personal Electronics and the Library** by Jason Griffey
May/June 48:4	**Linked Data Tools: Connecting on the Web** by Karen Coyle
July 48:5	**RFID in Libraries** by Lori Bowen Ayre
August/ September 48:6	**Running the Digital Branch: Guidelines for Operating the Library Website** by David Lee King
October 48:7	**Making the Library More Accessible through Technology** by Char Booth
November/ December 48:8	**Integrated Library Systems** by Marshall Breeding

ALA TechSource

alatechsource.org

ALA TechSource, a unit of the publishing department of the American Library Association